SIMPLY THE BEST
STEAMER RECIPES

MARIAN GETZ

ACKNOWLEDGMENTS

A most sincere thank you to our wonderful viewers and customers for without you there would be no need for a cookbook. I try very hard to give you an array of recipes suited for the particular kitchen tool the cookbook is written for. Wolfgang and I create recipes faster than we can write them down. That is what chefs do and is also the reason to tune in to the live shows and even record them so you can learn new dishes that may not be in our cookbooks yet.

Thank you most of all to Wolfgang. You are the most passionate chef I know and it has been a privilege to work for you since 1998. You are a great leader and friend. Your restaurants are full of cooks and staff that have been with you for 20 or more years which is a true testament to how you lead us. Thanks for allowing me to write these cookbooks and for letting me share the stage at HSN with you.

To Greg, my sweet husband since 1983. Working together is a dream and I love you. You have taught me what a treasure it is to have a home filled with people to laugh with.

To my sons, Jordan and Benjamin, we have a beautiful life, don't we? It just keeps on getting better since we added Lindsay, J.J. and now precious Easton, our first grandbaby.

To all the great people at WP Productions, Syd, Arnie, Mike, Phoebe, Nicolle, Michael, Genevieve and the rest of the team, you are all wonderful to work with.

To Daniel Koren, our patient editor and photographer, thank you for your dedication.

Thanks to our great team of very hard working people who pull off the live shows at HSN. It is a magical production to watch, from the first box unpacked, to the thousands of eggs cracked and beaten, to running to get that "thing" Wolf asks for at the last minute, to the very last dish washed and put away.

Most of us think of steaming food as a practice mostly used for preparing Asian dishes such as rice, pot stickers, vegetables and fish. Many of my restaurants use steamers for their versatility and simplicity. I created a steamer for the home cook to use and enjoy on an everyday basis and I have urged Marian to share her favorite recipes with as many people as possible through this cookbook.

Marian was thrilled when I asked her to write a cookbook to accompany the steamer. She loves Asian food as much as I do and instantly thought of dozens of recipes to include in this cookbook. She soon found out that steaming can be universal throughout all cooking cultures and used her knowledge to create recipes for any occasion.

A student of cooking is probably one of the best ways to describe Marian. She is always looking for something new, something fresh, something local and something seasonal. Her culinary knowledge combined with her passion for cooking is second to none. The recipes that Marian has written for this cookbook will motivate you to be more creative in the kitchen.

As I learned long ago, alongside my mother and grandmother, you should always put lots of love into everything you cook. This is certainly evident in this collection of Marian's steamer recipes.

INTRODUCTION BY WOLFGANG PUCK

DESSERTS

EXTRAS

STEAMER TIPS

Hot Steam

Please use caution when opening a lid or when stacking and un-stacking steamer baskets. Use thick oven mitts to protect your hands and forearms. Steam burns happen fast and are very painful.

Kitchen Towels

Place a kitchen towel or paper towels on the counter before un-stacking the steamer baskets after steaming is complete. There will be considerable moisture left on the counter from the baskets if you don't use a towel.

Additional Steaming Time

Food size, density and temperature can differ so steaming times may vary from the suggested steaming time in the recipes. If the food you are steaming is not done at the suggested steaming time, add a few more minutes to it. Depending on the length of time you have already been steaming, you may have to add more water to the water tank as well.

Delicate Foods

If you are steaming very delicate foods such as shrimp or custards, remember that the steam starts fastest and is slightly hotter in the bottom steamer basket. Pay attention to how fast delicate foods are steaming if using the bottom basket.

Meat Thermometer

When cooking meats, chicken, pork or fish, it is very helpful to have an accurate meat thermometer handy. A meat thermometer is the best way to prevent overcooking. I recommend an instant-read thermometer which can be purchased for less than $20.

Pureeing

Many of the foods in this book use an immersion blender to puree the finished foods. If you do not have one you can use a food processor, blender, food mill or even press the food through a sturdy strainer.

Steaming Baskets

The number of baskets to use for a given recipe depends on the size of the food and how it has been cut up. For this reason, all recipes will say to place the food into basket(s) so depending on your situation, use as many as needed to fit all your food.

Rice Tray

The Rice Tray refers to the bowl-like tray that comes with your steamer. It is very good for steaming juicy items or very small items that would otherwise fall through the grates of the steamer. You will find this accessory invaluable.

Testing For Doneness

For cakes, test for doneness by inserting a toothpick or bamboo skewer off-center. It should generally come out with just a few moist crumbs clinging to it. For custards, insert a knife off-center and it should come out clean. For breads, bake until the internal temperature registers approximately 200°F on a thermometer. For cookies, pizzas and pastries look for slight puffing and a brown color.

COOKING TIPS

Raw Meat

When cooking raw meat, be mindful of what you do with your tongs. If you use the same pair of tongs to place raw chicken in the steamer baskets then later use them to transfer the cooked chicken to a platter, there is a chance that those tongs may still have live bacteria on them. Either wash them before removing cooked food or use a second pair.

Know your Butcher

If you like to cook but are as busy as I am, I suggest you find a grocery store that still has a real butcher on premise. Make friends with your butcher as a good butcher will save you prep time in the kitchen and make you a better cook because of it. I have my butcher's phone number on speed dial in my phone.

Seasoning Your Food

When cooking savory foods, it is important to season it first. It can be as simple as salt alone or an elaborate array of spices and herbs. Season EVERY BITE of the food by sprinkling the seasonings evenly over the surface of the food. For me, salt and pepper do not always go together. Salt is by far the most important seasoning followed by something tart such as citrus, vinegar, wine, BBQ sauce or mustard that has a tartness to it. It's all about the right balance.

Prep Once - Use Twice

Think about any meals you may want to cook during the upcoming week and prep for more than you need today. For example, if you're chopping onions for today's meal, can you use the onions later in the week? If so, prep extra today and save time tomorrow.

Salt

The salt used in this book is Diamond Crystal Kosher Salt. It is half as salty as most other brands. This is because the grains are very fluffy and therefore not as many fit into a measuring spoon. This brand also lists only "salt" as the ingredient on the box. If you are using salt other than Diamond Crystal Kosher Salt, simply use half the amount specified in the recipe.

Butter

If a recipe calls for butter, I always use the unsalted kind. Salted butter has a longer shelf life as the salt acts as a preservative but it comes at the expense of a taste that is stale compared to that of unsalted butter. Softened butter means butter that has been left at room temperature for several hours. It should be soft enough to offer no resistance whatsoever when sliced using a knife. While there is no perfect substitute for the pure flavor of butter, you can use a substitute such as margarine and most of the recipes will turn out fairly well.

Vanilla

I adore vanilla and order both my vanilla extract and vanilla beans from a supplier directly from the island of Tahiti. I use both of these in recipes where the vanilla flavor takes center stage. In recipes where vanilla is not the star flavor, I use imitation vanilla because it is less expensive and adds the right amount of taste and aroma without overpowering the other flavors. My favorite is an inexpensive imitation flavoring called Magic Line Butter Vanilla Extract. It adds an incredible sweet smell and taste to baked goods.

Chocolate

Buy good quality chocolate and cocoa whenever possible. It is easy to find excellent chocolate at most grocery stores but it is almost impossible to find good quality cocoa powder. I suggest ordering it online.

Sugar Substitute

If you need to use a sugar substitute, my favorite kind is an all-natural product called Zsweet. I get it at my local health food store. While it does not bake as perfectly as regular sugar, it is the best substitute I know. I also like agave and stevia.

PANTRY TIPS

Being prepared to cook the recipes in this book, or any recipe for that matter, is one of the keys to success in the kitchen. Your pantry must be stocked with the basics. We all know how frustrating it can be when you go to the cupboard and what you need is not there. This list includes some of the ingredients you will find in this book and some that we feel are important to always have on hand.

Perishables:

Onions
Garlic
Tomatoes
Carrots
Celery
Ginger
Bell Peppers
White Potatoes
Sweet Potatoes
Squashes
Citrus
Apples
Bananas
Lettuce
Spinach
Fresh Herbs
Green Onions
Milk
Cream Cheese
Parmesan Cheese
Yogurt
Other Cheeses You Like

Spices:

Kosher Salt
Pepper
Bay Leaves
Sage
Oregano
Thyme
Chili Flakes
Cumin Seeds
Curry Powder
Onion Powder
Garlic Powder
Dry Mustard
Ground Cinnamon
Nutmeg
Cloves
Chili Powder

Dry goods:

Sugars
Sugar Substitute
Vanilla
Extracts/Flavorings
Agave Syrup
Canned Tomatoes
Canned Beans
Canned Vegetables
Dried Chilies
Pasta
Lentils
Stocks
Powdered Bouillon
Olives
Ketchup
Mustard
Pickles
Oils
Vinegar
Honey

It is not necessary to have all the items listed at all times. However, if you are feeling creative, adventurous or just following a recipe, it's great to have a good selection in the kitchen.

CHICKEN WITH
PEANUT SAUCE

Makes 4 servings

For The Chicken:

6 boneless, skinless chicken thighs

4 cups ice water

4 teaspoons kosher salt or 2 teaspoons other salt

2 tablespoons yellow onions, finely chopped

2 tablespoons fresh cilantro, finely chopped

For The Peanut Dipping Sauce:

2 garlic cloves, minced

3 tablespoons peanut butter, melted in microwave

2 teaspoons light brown sugar

1 teaspoon bottled sriracha or hot sauce

1 tablespoon tomato paste

2 tablespoons chicken stock

2 tablespoons hoisin sauce

2 tablespoons peanuts, chopped

Method:

1. *Cut each chicken thigh into 1-inch cubes and place in a mixing bowl.*
2. *Add the ice water and salt to the bowl; stir to dissolve the salt.*
3. *Let rest for 15 minutes then transfer chicken to steamer basket(s).*
4. *Fill water tank with water.*
5. *Cover steamer and set timer to 5 minutes.*
6. *Steam for 5 minutes or until internal temperature registers 165°F on a meat thermometer.*
7. *Remove then toss with the onions and cilantro in a bowl.*
8. *In a separate bowl, combine all dipping sauce ingredients; stir.*
9. *Serve chicken with dipping sauce.*

GARLIC
CHICKEN THIGHS

Makes 4 servings

Ingredients:

6 boneless, skinless chicken thighs

3 garlic cloves, minced

2 green onions, chopped

1 teaspoon dried thyme

1 tablespoon unsalted butter

Kosher salt and fresh pepper taste

Cooked rice or pasta for serving

Method:

1. *In a bowl, combine all ingredients, except rice or pasta; toss to coat chicken thoroughly.*
2. *Place chicken thighs on a piece of aluminum foil (big enough to make a pouch).*
3. *Fold the foil then seal on all sides.*
4. *Fill water tank with water.*
5. *Place foil pouch in the bottom steamer basket.*
6. *Cut 4 small holes in the top of the foil using a small knife.*
7. *Cover steamer and set timer to 10 minutes.*
8. *Steam for 8-10 minutes or until internal temperature of the chicken reaches 165°F on a meat thermometer.*
9. *When steaming is complete, carefully remove the pouch and let rest for 5 minutes.*
10. *Tear open foil pouch and serve chicken with rice or pasta.*

ALTON'S
BUFFALO WINGS

Makes 4 appetizer servings

Ingredients:

12 whole chicken wings, cut into 24 pieces, excluding tips

6 tablespoons unsalted butter

1 small garlic clove, minced

¼ cup bottled hot pepper sauce

½ teaspoon kosher salt

Method:

1. *Fill water tank with water.*

2. *Arrange the wings in steamer basket(s).*

3. *Cover steamer and set timer to 10 minutes.*

4. *When steaming is complete, remove wings and pat dry using paper towels.*

5. *Spread wings out on a cooling rack over paper towels set on a ½ sheet pan.*

6. *Refrigerate for 1 hour.*

7. *Preheat oven to 425°F.*

8. *Replace paper towels with parchment paper underneath the cooling rack.*

9. *Roast on the middle rack of the oven for 20 minutes.*

10. *Turn wings over and roast for an additional 20 minutes or until wings are cooked through and golden brown.*

11. *While wings are roasting, microwave the butter and garlic in a small microwave-safe bowl until butter is melted.*

12. *Pour butter mixture and remaining ingredients into a bowl large enough to hold all of the chicken wings; stir to combine.*

13. *Remove the wings from the oven then transfer to the bowl.*

14. *Toss well until coated and serve immediately.*

TIP

Steaming the wings first and later roasting them results in a much jucier and crispy appetizer.

CURRIED CHICKEN
WITH BOK CHOY

Makes 4 servings

Ingredients:

4 cups cold water

1 cup ice cubes

4 teaspoons kosher salt

4 boneless, skinless chicken breasts

1 tablespoon curry powder

1 teaspoon ground turmeric

2 tablespoons cream of coconut

1 teaspoon powdered chicken bouillon

2 teaspoons fresh ginger, minced

1 garlic clove, minced

2 small bunches bok choy, split (or broccoli)

1 green onion, finely sliced

Method:

1. *In a large bowl, combine the water and ice cubes.*

2. *Whisk in the salt (the water should taste like sea water, add more salt if needed); whisk until salt is dissolved.*

3. *Place the chicken into the brine and let stand for 1 hour.*

4. *In a small bowl, combine the curry, turmeric, coconut, bouillon, ginger and garlic.*

5. *Remove the chicken from the brine, pat dry then spread thoroughly with curry mixture.*

6. *Fill water tank with water.*

7. *Arrange chicken in the bottom and middle steamer baskets.*

8. *Arrange the bok choy in the top steamer basket.*

9. *Cover steamer and set timer to 8 minutes.*

10. *Steam for 6-8 minutes or until internal temperature of the chicken just reaches 165°F on a meat thermometer; remove immediately.*

11. *At this time, the bok choy should be crisp tender as well.*

12. *Remove and slice the chicken into ¼-inch thick slices.*

13. *Garnish with green onions and serve with the bok choy.*

TIP

For a nice spice kick, add 2-3 teaspoons Sriracha chili paste to the curry mixture.

16

CHINESE-STYLE CHICKEN SALAD

Makes 4 servings

Ingredients:

4 boneless, skinless chicken breasts, cut into 1-inch cubes

8 cups ice water

2 tablespoons + 2 teaspoons kosher salt (or half that amount if using other salt)

3 cups iceberg lettuce, shredded

1 carrot, finely julienned

1 bunch green onions, thinly sliced

1 Granny Smith apple, julienned

½ cup roasted peanuts, chopped

½ cup cilantro leaves

3 tablespoons dry mustard

4 tablespoons rice wine vinegar

½ cup canola oil

2 tablespoons honey

1 tablespoon soy sauce

1 teaspoon dark sesame oil

Method:

1. *In a bowl, combine the chicken, ice water and salt; let brine for 15 minutes.*
2. *Drain then divide the chicken evenly between the steamer baskets.*
3. *Cover steamer and set timer to 5 minutes.*
4. *Steam for 4-5 minutes or until internal temperature reaches 165°F on a meat thermometer.*
5. *Remove and set aside.*
6. *In a bowl, combine the lettuce, carrots, green onions, apples, peanuts and cilantro; toss.*
7. *In a separate bowl, whisk together the remaining ingredients.*
8. *Add the chicken to the salad bowl then drizzle with as much dressing as desired.*
9. *Serve while chicken is warm.*

CHICKEN SALAD

Makes 4 servings

Ingredients:

4 boneless, skinless chicken breasts

½ celery stalk, diced

¼ medium red onion, diced

¼ Golden Delicious apple, quartered then cut into thin slices

¼ cup raisins

¼ cup red seedless grapes, halved

2 tablespoons sweet pickle relish

½ cup mayonnaise

1 tablespoon yellow mustard

1 teaspoon kosher salt

½ teaspoon fresh pepper

½ teaspoon lemon juice

Method:

1. *Fill water tank with water.*
2. *Place the chicken breasts in steamer basket(s).*
3. *Cover steamer and set timer to 8 minutes.*
4. *Steam for 6-8 minutes or until internal temperature reaches 165°F on a meat thermometer.*
5. *While steaming, combine remaining ingredients in a bowl using a spoon.*
6. *When steaming is complete, let rest for 5 minutes.*
7. *Transfer the chicken breasts to a cutting board then slice into ¾-inch squares.*
8. *Add chicken to the bowl; toss well.*
9. *Garnish as desired and serve.*

BBQ TURKEY
TENDERLOINS

Makes 4 servings

Ingredients:

2 turkey tenderloins
2 tablespoons BBQ flavored dry rub
Bottled BBQ sauce

Method:

1. *Place the tenderloins on a cutting board and apply the dry rub all over.*
2. *Fill water tank with water.*
3. *Place the tenderloins in steamer basket(s).*
4. *Cover steamer and set timer to 15 minutes.*
5. *Steam for 12-15 minutes or until internal temperature of the tenderloins reaches 165°F on a meat thermometer.*
6. *When steaming is complete, remove then cut into ½-inch thick medallions.*
7. *Top with BBQ sauce and serve immediately.*

TIP

If you like sweet BBQ sauce but need to avoid excess sugar, use a BBQ sauce without sugar and stir in some Zsweet sweetener. It has by far the least aftertaste of any of the zero-calorie sweeteners available.

BEEF &
NOODLES

Makes 4 servings

Ingredients:

1½ pounds beef chuck roast

2 tablespoons soy sauce

1 tablespoon powdered beef bouillon

1 teaspoon fresh black pepper

1 teaspoon onion powder

1 teaspoon garlic powder

1 teaspoon paprika

1 tablespoon tomato paste

¾ cup water

1 pound pasta, cooked

Method:

1. *Cut the beef into 3/4-inch cubes then transfer to a mixing bowl.*
2. *In a separate bowl, combine remaining ingredients, except pasta; stir.*
3. *Add half of the sauce to the beef; toss until beef is coated thoroughly.*
4. *Fill water tank with water.*
5. *Place the beef in the bottom steamer basket.*
6. *Cover steamer and set timer to 30 minutes.*
7. *Steam for 30 minutes or until beef is fork tender.*
8. *Place remaining sauce in a large sauté pan over medium heat during the last 5 minutes of the beef steaming.*
9. *Add the pasta to the sauté pan and toss to coat.*
10. *Add the beef to the sauté pan; stir.*
11. *Remove, garnish as desired and serve immediately.*

BEST POT ROAST &
VEGGIES

Makes 4 servings

Ingredients:

1½ pounds beef chuck roast

2 tablespoons soy sauce

1 tablespoon powdered beef bouillon

1 teaspoon fresh black pepper

1 teaspoon onion powder

1 teaspoon garlic powder

1 teaspoon paprika

1 tablespoon tomato paste

1 medium yellow onion, quartered

8 red bliss potatoes

2 carrots, cut into rounds

1 celery stalk, cut into large pieces

Method:

1. *Cut beef into 1/2-inch thick steaks and place in a bowl.*

2. *In a separate small bowl, stir together the soy sauce, bouillon, pepper, onion powder, garlic powder, paprika and tomato paste; reserve half of the flavoring mixture.*

3. *Stir half of the flavoring mixture into the beef and smear to coat each side; let rest for 30 minutes.*

4. *Fill water tank with water.*

5. *Arrange meat in steamer basket(s).*

6. *Cover steamer and set timer to 30 minutes.*

7. *When steaming is complete, refill the water tank if needed and set timer for an additional 15 minutes or until fork tender.*

8. *Add remaining vegetables to the other two steamer baskets and steam for an additional 15 minutes or until potatoes are tender; remove to a serving platter.*

9. *Brush meat with reserved flavoring mixture and serve with vegetables.*

STEAK, BLUE CHEESE & SPINACH SALAD

Makes 4 servings

Ingredients:

2 sirloin steaks, 4-5 ounces each

2 tablespoons soy sauce

2 teaspoons Worcestershire sauce

2 garlic cloves, minced

1 teaspoon fresh pepper

1 tablespoon dry mustard

8 cups baby spinach

½ cup grape tomatoes, halved

1 small red onion, sliced very thinly

2 ounces blue cheese, crumbled

2 ounces walnuts, toasted and chopped

1 ripe Bartlett pear, diced

Kosher salt and fresh pepper to taste

Vinaigrette dressing of your choice

Method:

1. *Place beef on a plate.*

2. *In a bowl, combine the soy sauce, Worcestershire sauce, garlic, pepper and mustard.*

3. *Brush mixture all over the beef; let rest for 15 minutes.*

4. *Fill water tank with water.*

5. *Place the beef in steamer basket(s).*

6. *Cover steamer and set timer to 5 minutes if you prefer your meat medium-rare (add an additional 1-2 minutes for more well done meat).*

7. *Steam for 5 minutes or until desired doneness.*

8. *When steaming is complete, remove beef and let cool for 5 minutes.*

9. *In a bowl, toss remaining ingredients together.*

10. *Slice steaks very thinly against the grain and place on top of the salad before serving.*

DELICIOUS MEATBALLS

Makes 2 servings

Ingredients:

1 pound lean ground beef

¼ cup white onions, finely chopped

½ cup breadcrumbs

2 tablespoons whole milk

2 teaspoons Italian seasoning

2 teaspoons fresh parsley, chopped

1 teaspoon Worcestershire sauce

Kosher salt and fresh pepper to taste

Tomato sauce or BBQ sauce for serving

Method:

1. *In a bowl, combine all ingredients, except tomato or BBQ sauce; mix well.*
2. *Divide the mixture into 8 portions.*
3. *Form each portion into a ball using your hands.*
4. *Fill water tank with water.*
5. *Place the meatballs in the top steamer basket.*
6. *Cover steamer and set timer to 15 minutes.*
7. *Steam for 12-15 minutes or until internal temperature reaches 165°F on a meat thermometer.*
8. *When steaming is complete, serve with your favorite tomato or BBQ sauce.*

TIP

Try using other types of ground meat such as meatloaf mix which is available at many meat counters (it is a mixture of beef, veal and pork). For a healthier option, substitute 1/2 lb. of ground beef with ground bison.

DINER DOGS WITH SAUERKRAUT

Makes 4 servings

Ingredients:

4 jumbo hot dogs

2 cups sauerkraut

4 hot dog buns

Spicy mustard for serving

Method:

1. *Fill water tank with water.*
2. *Place the hot dogs in the bottom steamer basket.*
3. *Place the sauerkraut in the middle steamer basket.*
4. *Cover steamer and set timer to 4 minutes.*
5. *Steam for 3-4 minutes or until the internal temperature of hot dogs reaches 160°F on a meat thermometer.*
6. *Place hot dog buns in the top steamer basket using tongs during the last 20 seconds of steaming.*
7. *When steaming is complete, place steamer baskets on towels to drain.*
8. *Assemble hot dogs, top with mustard and serve.*

TIP

Buy sauerkraut in bags from the deli or refrigerated section of your grocery store. The flavor is much fresher than what you will find in a can.

CIDER BRINED
PORK CHOPS

Makes 4 servings

Ingredients:

4 cups apple cider

4 teaspoons kosher salt

¼ cup brown sugar

2 cups beer

4 boneless pork chops, cut 1-inch thick

Method:

1. *In a bowl, combine the apple cider, salt and sugar; whisk until sugar and salt have dissolved.*

2. *Add the beer and gently stir to combine.*

3. *Place the pork chops into the mixture then cover with plastic wrap.*

4. *Refrigerate for 4-8 hours or overnight.*

5. *Fill water tank with water.*

6. *Remove pork chops from the bowl and pat dry.*

7. *Place the pork chops in steamer basket(s).*

8. *Cover steamer and set timer to 9 minutes.*

9. *Steam for 7-9 minutes or until internal temperature reaches 155°F on a meat thermometer.*

10. *When steaming is complete, remove and serve immediately.*

PORK CHOPS WITH
APPLE BUTTER

Makes 4 servings

For The Brine:

4 cups cold water

1 cup ice cubes

2 teaspoons salt + more if needed

For The Pork Chops:

4 center cut loin pork chops, 1-inch thick

1 Granny Smith apple, cut into wedges

1 Pink Lady apple, cut into wedges

Kosher salt and fresh pepper to taste

½ cup jarred apple butter

1 tablespoon balsamic vinegar

Method:

1. In a large bowl, combine the water and ice cubes.
2. Whisk in the salt (the water should taste like sea water, add more salt if needed); whisk until salt is dissolved.
3. Place the pork chops into the brine and let stand for 1 hour.
4. Fill water tank with water.
5. Arrange the pork chops in the bottom and middle steamer baskets.
6. Arrange the apple wedges in the top steamer basket.
7. Cover steamer and set timer to 8 minutes.
8. Steam for 6-8 minutes or until internal temperature just reaches 150°F on a meat thermometer.
9. Remove pork chops immediately then season with salt and pepper.
10. Remove apples and add to the pork chops.
11. Stir together the apple butter and balsamic vinegar then brush on both sides of each pork chop.
12. Drizzle any remaining apple butter mixture over the apples and serve.

TIP

For extra flavor drizzle the steamed apple wedges with a little melted butter and sprinkle with cinnamon and sugar before serving.

JUICY BRINED
SHRIMP

Makes 4 servings

For The Shrimp:

1-1½ pounds large shrimp, thawed, peeled & deveined

7 cups cold water

1 cup ice cubes

8 teaspoons kosher salt (or 4 teaspoons other salt)

For The Mustard Sauce:

2 tablespoons spicy brown mustard

2 tablespoons sour cream or yogurt

2 tablespoons apple cider vinegar

Kosher salt and fresh pepper to taste

1 small garlic clove, minced

2 tablespoons fresh parsley, chopped

Method:

1. *In a large bowl, combine all shrimp ingredients.*
2. *Stir to dissolve the salt and let stand for 15 minutes.*
3. *Fill water tank with water.*
4. *Drain shrimp and place in steamer basket(s).*
5. *Cover steamer and set timer to 4 minutes.*
6. *Steam for 3-4 minutes or until shrimp just turns pink (monitor the shrimp while steaming, they turn pink quickly).*
7. *When steaming is complete, transfer the shrimp to a serving platter.*
8. *In a small bowl, stir together all mustard sauce ingredients.*
9. *Serve shrimp with mustard sauce.*

SHRIMP WITH SPICY
COCKTAIL SAUCE

Makes 4 servings

For The Shrimp:

4 cups water

4 teaspoons kosher salt + more if needed

1 pound large shrimp (11-15 count)

For The Cocktail Sauce:

¾ cup ketchup

¼ cup prepared horseradish

1 teaspoon Worcestershire

½ teaspoon bottled hot chili pepper sauce

¼ teaspoon kosher salt

¼ teaspoon fresh pepper

¼ teaspoon lemon zest

1 tablespoon lemon juice

Method:

1. *In a bowl, combine the water and salt (the water should taste like sea water, add more salt if needed); whisk until salt is dissolved.*
2. *Place shrimp in the salt water and let stand for 1 hour.*
3. *Fill water tank with water.*
4. *Place the shrimp in steamer basket(s).*
5. *Cover steamer and set timer to 5 minutes.*
6. *Steam for 4-5 minutes or until shrimp are pink in color.*
7. *In a bowl, stir together all cocktail sauce ingredients.*
8. *Serve shrimp with cocktail sauce.*

SHRIMP SALAD

Makes 4 servings

Ingredients:

1 pound small shrimp (31-35 count), peeled and deveined

¾ cup mayonnaise

¼ small red onion, chopped

2 green onions, chopped

1 celery stalk, diced

1 tablespoon fresh dill, chopped

2 tablespoons sweet pickle relish

Kosher salt and fresh pepper to taste

Method:

1. *Fill water tank with water.*

2. *Place shrimp in the top steamer basket.*

3. *Cover steamer and set timer to 3 minutes.*

4. *Steam for 2-3 minutes or until shrimp turn pink in color.*

5. *When steaming is complete, transfer shrimp to a towel lined plate and place in the refrigerator.*

6. *In a bowl, combine remaining ingredients.*

7. *Once shrimp have cooled, add to the mixture; stir.*

8. *Serve cold.*

TIP

You can substitute Greek yogurt for the mayonnaise if you want to reduce calories. Be sure not to overcook the shrimp, they will be rubbery if overcooked.

MISO RUBBED

COD

Makes 2 servings

Ingredients:

1 tablespoon white miso paste

2 teaspoons soy sauce

2 teaspoons honey

1 teaspoons bottled sriracha or other hot chili pepper sauce

2 green onions, thinly sliced

2 cod fillets, at least 1-inch thick

1 package (4 ounces) shiitake mushroom caps

Steamed brown or white rice, for serving

Method:

1. *In a small bowl, stir together the miso, soy sauce, honey, hot sauce and green onions.*
2. *Place the cod fillets on a plate.*
3. *Brush mixture on all sides of the cod fillets and mushrooms.*
4. *Let stand for 10 minutes.*
5. *Fill water tank with water.*
6. *Arrange the cod fillets and mushrooms together in steamer basket(s).*
7. *Cover steamer and set timer to 8 minutes.*
8. *Steam for 5-8 minutes or until cod is just cooked through.*
9. *When steaming is complete, serve cod with steamed rice.*

TIP

Make this a whole meal by steaming green cabbage wedges in the remaining space of the steamer baskets for the same 5-8 minutes.

PESTO STEAMED
SALMON FILLETS

Makes 2 servings

Ingredients:

1 medium yellow onion, sliced into rings

2 center-cut salmon fillets

2 tablespoons jarred pesto + more for serving

Kosher salt and fresh pepper to taste

1 lemon, sliced into wheels

4 cups fresh baby spinach

Method:

1. *Fill water tank with water.*
2. *Arrange onions and salmon fillets in the bottom steamer basket.*
3. *Spread each salmon fillet with a tablespoon of pesto.*
4. *Season with salt and pepper.*
5. *Place a lemon wheel on top of each salmon fillet.*
6. *Cover steamer and set timer to 6 minutes.*
7. *Steam for 4 minutes then add the spinach to the remaining steamer basket(s) for the last 2 minutes of steaming.*
8. *When steaming is complete, test for desired doneness then season again with salt and pepper.*
9. *Serve immediately with remaining lemon wheels and additional pesto.*

LOBSTER TAILS WITH
HERBED BUTTER

Makes 2 servings

Ingredients:

½ cup (1 stick) unsalted butter, room temperature

¼ teaspoon lemon zest

2 teaspoons fresh lemon juice

1 teaspoon fresh dill, finely chopped

1 teaspoon fresh parsley, finely chopped

1 green onion, finely chopped

Kosher salt and fresh pepper to taste

2 lobster tails (8-10 ounces each)

Method:

1. *In a bowl, combine all ingredients, except lobster tails.*
2. *Place the butter mixture on a piece of plastic wrap.*
3. *Form the butter mixture into a log then wrap it tightly.*
4. *Refrigerate for 2 hours or until firm.*
5. *Cut log into ¼-inch thick coins.*
6. *Fill water tank with water.*
7. *Arrange the lobster tails in the top steamer basket.*
8. *Cover steamer and set timer to 12 minutes.*
9. *Steam for 10-12 minutes or until the meat is firm and no longer translucent.*
10. *Remove from steamer then take the meat out of the shells.*
11. *Slice into ½-inch thick medallions, top with herbed butter and serve.*

TIP
You can use frozen lobster tails
by adding 8-10 minutes
of steaming time.

SEA BASS & SPAGHETTI SQUASH

Makes 2 servings

Ingredients:

2 thick sea bass fillets, corvina or other firm fish

1 tablespoon mayonnaise or yogurt

1 garlic clove, minced

1 green onion, thinly sliced

1 teaspoon fresh thyme leaves

Kosher salt and fresh pepper to taste

1 small spaghetti squash, halved

½ pound fresh baby spinach, washed

Melted butter, for serving (optional)

Method:

1. *Place fish on a plate.*

2. *In a small bowl, stir together the mayonnaise, garlic, green onions, thyme, salt and pepper.*

3. *Spread mixture on all sides of the fish; let rest for 10 minutes.*

4. *While fish rests, prepare the squash by removing the seeds and loose strings.*

5. *Place the squash in steamer basket(s).*

6. *Fill water tank with water.*

7. *Cover steamer and set timer to 10 minutes.*

8. *When steaming is complete, check squash for tenderness, it should still need more steaming time (keep basket on the steamer).*

9. *Add fish to the middle steamer basket and steam for 5-7 minutes or until translucent.*

10. *Add the spinach to the top steamer basket and steam for 2 minutes or until just wilted.*

11. *Remove each steamer basket as food is done.*

12. *Drizzle spaghetti squash with a bit of the butter, season with salt and pepper then use a fork to pull the long strands of "spaghetti" from the squash.*

13. *Serve immediately.*

STEAMED HALIBUT
WITH RICE

Makes 2 servings

Ingredients:

2 cups dry jasmine or basmati rice

4 carrots, julienned

2 cups snow peas, julienned

1 bunch green onions, julienned

1 red bell pepper, julienned

Kosher salt and fresh pepper to taste

4 pieces halibut, 4 ounces each

2 teaspoons fresh ginger, minced

2 garlic cloves, minced

2 teaspoons sesame seeds

Method:

1. *On your stovetop, bring a tea kettle or pot of water to a boil.*
2. *Place rice in the rice tray and season with salt if desired.*
3. *Pour boiling water over the level rice until it is ½-inch higher than the rice.*
4. *Fill water tank with water.*
5. *Carefully place the rice tray in the bottom steamer basket.*
6. *Cover steamer and set timer to 30 minutes.*
7. *Arrange vegetables in layers in the middle steamer basket; season with salt and pepper then set aside.*
8. *Place halibut in the top steamer basket and sprinkle with ginger, garlic, salt, pepper and sesame seeds.*
9. *When rice has 5 minutes to go, add the middle vegetable basket and top halibut basket to the steamer; let cook for the remaining 5 minutes.*
10. *Fish should be opaque and just cooked through when finished steaming.*
11. *Carefully remove all steamer baskets.*
12. *Fluff the rice and scoop onto a serving platter.*
13. *Top with the vegetables and lay the halibut on top.*
14. *Serve immediately.*

TUNA WITH SESAME SEEDS

Makes 2 servings

Ingredients:

1 teaspoon dark sesame oil

2 teaspoons soy sauce

1 teaspoon honey

1 teaspoon fresh ginger, minced

1 fresh garlic clove, minced

2 fresh tuna steaks, sushi grade, 4 ounces each

1 tablespoons black (or white) sesame seeds

1 pound fresh green beans, trimmed

Method:

1. *In a small bowl, whisk together the sesame oil, soy sauce, honey, ginger and garlic.*

2. *Place the tuna on a plate and pour soy mixture over the tuna.*

3. *Turn tuna on all sides to evenly coat with soy mixture.*

4. *Let stand for 10 minutes, turning often.*

5. *Sprinkle tuna evenly with sesame seeds and press onto the fish.*

6. *Fill water tank with water.*

7. *Place the tuna in the bottom steamer basket.*

8. *Place the green beans in the other steamer basket(s).*

9. *Cover steamer and set timer to 3 minutes.*

10. *Steam for 3 minutes or until tuna just turns opaque on the exterior.*

11. *When steaming is complete, remove immediately to serving plates.*

12. *Taste a green bean, if it is still too crunchy, steam for an additional 1-2 minutes.*

13. *Cut tuna into attractive slices and fan out on plates.*

14. *Remove green beans and serve with tuna.*

TIP

Carrots also go well with this dish. If you want to add a little spice, pick up a tube of wasabi paste from the grocery store's sushi case and top each tuna steak with a little of it.

ACORN SQUASH

Makes 4 servings

Ingredients:

1 acorn squash, cut into 1-inch rings

¼ cup brown sugar

Pinch of ground cinnamon

Pinch of kosher salt

2 tablespoons unsalted butter

Method:

1. *Fill water tank with water.*

2. *Place the squash in steamer basket(s).*

3. *Sprinkle squash with sugar, a pinch of cinnamon and salt.*

4. *Cover steamer and set timer to 18 minutes.*

5. *Steam for 18 minutes or until fork tender.*

6. *When steaming is complete, remove, brush with butter, garnish as desired and serve.*

TIP

Sometimes I serve this dish topped with crushed up cinnamon red hot candies.

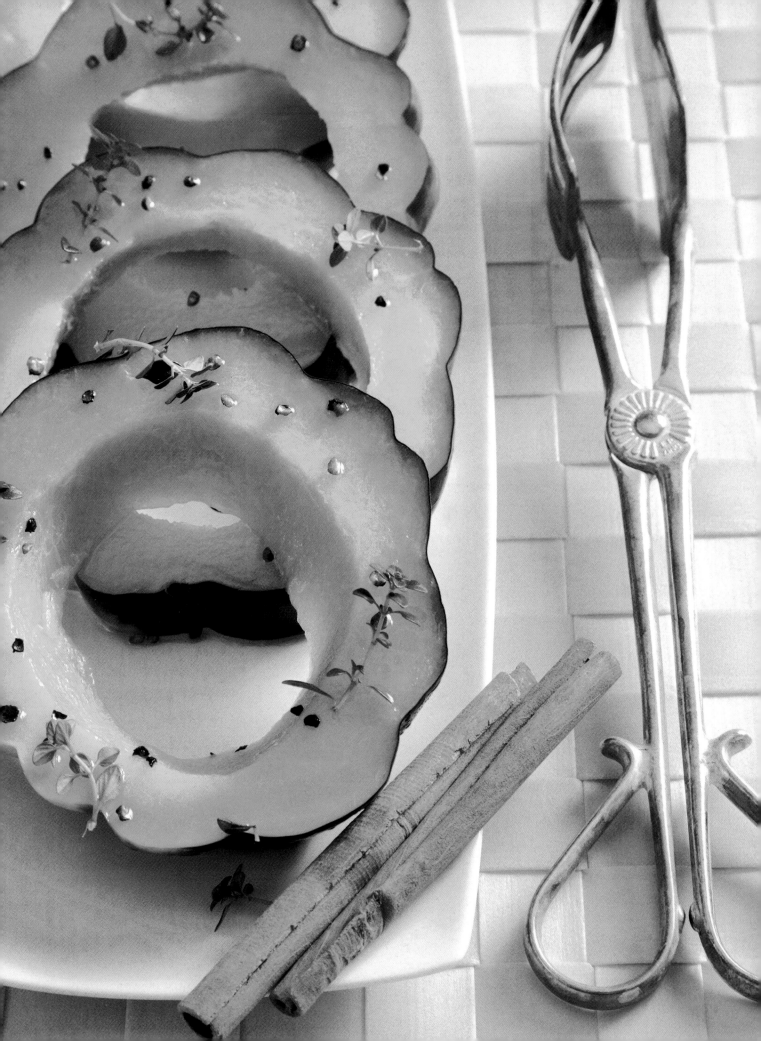

CARROTS WITH CILANTRO & LIME

Makes 4 servings

Ingredients:

1¼ pounds small carrots

1 tablespoon unsalted butter, melted

2 teaspoons fresh lime juice

Kosher salt and fresh pepper to taste

1 tablespoon fresh cilantro, chopped

Method:

1. *Fill water tank with water.*

2. *Place carrots in the top steamer basket.*

3. *Cover steamer and set timer to 20 minutes.*

4. *Steam for 18-20 minutes or until carrots are tender.*

5. *When steaming is complete, transfer the carrots to a serving bowl.*

6. *Toss with butter, lime juice, salt and pepper.*

7. *Garnish with cilantro and serve immediately.*

TIP

If you don't like cilantro try an herb that you do like.
Some chopped sage goes wonderfully
with these sweet carrots.

BOK CHOY WITH SESAME DRESSING

Makes 4 servings

Ingredients:

1 teaspoon sesame oil

½ teaspoon granulated sugar

1 tablespoon soy sauce

1 garlic clove, minced

1-inch piece of fresh ginger, minced

¼ teaspoon crushed red pepper

4 bok choy, cut in half

Sesame seeds, for serving

Method:

1. *To make the sesame dressing, combine all ingredients, except bok choy and sesame seeds, in a bowl; whisk until the sugar has dissolved then set aside.*

2. *Fill water tank with water.*

3. *Place the bok choy in steamer basket(s).*

4. *Cover steamer and set timer to 4 minutes.*

5. *Steam for 3-4 minutes or until the whites of the stems are tender.*

6. *Remove bok choy to a serving plate.*

7. *Drizzle with sesame dressing and garnish as desired before serving.*

TIP

If you can't find baby bok choy you can use the larger size that is more commonly available or substitute with Napa cabbage.

LEMON ASPARAGUS

Makes 4 servings

For The Asparagus:

1 pound asparagus spears, trimmed

For The Vinaigrette:

1 teaspoon fresh lemon zest

1 tablespoon fresh lemon juice

1 teaspoon Dijon mustard

1 tablespoon olive oil

Kosher salt and fresh pepper to taste

Method:

1. *Fill water tank with water.*
2. *Place the asparagus in steamer basket(s).*
3. *Cover steamer and set timer to 5 minutes.*
4. *Steam for 4-5 minutes or until asparagus are tender.*
5. *When steaming is complete, remove the asparagus to a serving plate.*
6. *In a bowl, combine all vinaigrette ingredients; whisk well.*
7. *Drizzle the vinaigrette over the asparagus and serve.*

EASY
BORSCHT

Makes 6 servings

Ingredients:

2 pounds fresh beets, scrubbed

1 yellow onion, chopped

6 cups water

¼ cup vinegar

¼ cup granulated sugar

2 teaspoons kosher salt

¼ cup heavy cream

¾ cup sour cream

2 tablespoons fresh dill

Method:

1. *Fill water tank with water.*

2. *Place the beets in steamer basket(s).*

3. *Cover steamer and set timer to 30 minutes.*

4. *Steam for 30 minutes or until beets are tender.*

5. *Place remaining ingredients, except sour cream and dill in a bowl then add the beets.*

6. *Purée using an immersion blender until smooth.*

7. *Taste and adjust seasoning if desired.*

8. *Ladle into bowls and garnish with sour cream and dill before serving.*

BROCCOLI, CASHEWS & LEMON

Makes 4 servings

Ingredients:

1 pound broccoli florets

1 teaspoon lemon zest

2 teaspoons fresh lemon juice

2 tablespoons unsalted butter, melted

¼ teaspoon crushed red pepper

Kosher salt and fresh pepper to taste

¼ cup cashews, crushed

Method:

1. *Fill water tank with water.*
2. *Place the broccoli in steamer basket(s).*
3. *Cover steamer and set timer to 4 minutes.*
4. *Steam for 3-4 minutes or until just tender.*
5. *When steaming is complete, place steamer basket(s) on a towel to drain.*
6. *In a bowl, combine remaining ingredients, except cashews.*
7. *Transfer broccoli to the bowl and toss gently to coat.*
8. *Sprinkle with cashews and serve immediately.*

TIP

Try leaving all of the broccoli stalks intact and use a vegetable peeler to remove the outer layer. The stems taste wonderful and are a waste to throw away.

STEAMED ARTICHOKES WITH LEMON

Makes 4 servings

For The Artichokes:

4 large artichokes

1 lemon, sliced into rounds

For The Dipping Sauce:

⅓ cup mayonnaise, regular or low-fat

2 tablespoons sour cream or yogurt

¼ teaspoon fresh lemon zest

1 tablespoon fresh lemon juice

1 tablespoon chicken stock

1 tablespoon chives, minced

Method:

1. *Trim off the stem and top 1-inch of each artichoke.*
2. *Trim the spines off of each petal using scissors.*
3. *Arrange the artichokes in steamer basket(s).*
4. *Scatter lemon slices over the artichokes.*
5. *Fill water tank with water.*
6. *Cover steamer and set timer to 30 minutes.*
7. *While steaming, make the dipping sauce by stirring together all sauce ingredients in a small bowl.*
8. *When steaming is complete, check for doneness using a pair of tongs, the leaves should pull away easily.*
9. *Serve artichokes hot or cold with dipping sauce.*

LEEKS WITH BREADCRUMBS

Makes 4 servings

Ingredients:

4 large leeks
½ cup good-quality chicken stock
Kosher salt and fresh pepper to taste
1 teaspoon granulated sugar
4 tablespoons unsalted butter, divided
1 cup breadcrumbs from fresh bread
1 tablespoon fresh parsley, chopped

Method:

1. *Trim and slice the leeks lengthwise in half then crosswise into 1-inch pieces.*
2. *Place leeks in a strainer and rinse very well.*
3. *Drain leeks well then place in the rice tray.*
4. *Add the chicken stock, salt, pepper, sugar and half of the butter.*
5. *Fill water tank with water.*
6. *Place the rice tray in the bottom steamer basket.*
7. *Cover steamer and set timer to 30 minutes.*
8. *While steaming, preheat the oven to 350°F.*
9. *Melt remaining butter in the microwave then toss with the breadcrumbs.*
10. *Stir to coat evenly then season with salt and pepper.*
11. *Spread breadcrumbs out on a parchment-lined sheet pan.*
12. *Bake for 10-15 minutes or until golden brown; remove then stir in the parsley.*
13. *When steaming the leeks is complete, carefully remove and pour into a serving dish.*
14. *Sprinkle evenly with breadcrumbs and serve immediately.*

ZUCCHINI & YELLOW SQUASH

Makes 4 servings

Ingredients:

4 small zucchini, trimmed

4 small yellow squash

2 tablespoons unsalted butter, melted

Kosher salt and fresh pepper to taste

Method:

1. *Cut zucchini and squash into ¾-inch half moons.*
2. *Fill water tank with water.*
3. *Place zucchini and squash in steamer basket(s).*
4. *Cover steamer and set timer to 8 minutes.*
5. *Steam for 7-8 minutes or until tender.*
6. *When steaming is complete, place steamer basket(s) on a towel to drain.*
7. *Transfer zucchini and squash to a mixing bowl.*
8. *Drizzle with melted butter then season with salt and pepper.*
9. *Serve immediately.*

TIP

To make this a juicier side dish, steam a few tomatoes along with the zucchini and yellow squash. After steaming, chop the tomatoes and let their juices make a nice sauce for the vegetables.

BRUSSELS SPROUTS WITH BACON

Makes 4 servings

Ingredients:

1 pound Brussels sprouts, trimmed and halved

Kosher salt and fresh pepper to taste

3 bacon slices, chopped

Method:

1. *Fill water tank with water.*

2. *Place Brussels sprouts in steamer basket(s).*

3. *Season with salt and pepper.*

4. *Cover steamer and set timer to 6 minutes.*

5. *Steam for 5-6 minutes or until just tender.*

6. *When steaming is complete, place steamer basket(s) on a towel to drain.*

7. *In a saucepan over medium heat, sauté the bacon until slightly crisp.*

8. *Remove all but 1 tablespoon of bacon grease, leaving the bacon in the pan.*

9. *With the pan still warm, add the Brussels sprouts and toss to coat.*

10. *Serve immediately.*

TIP

If you are pressed for time, you can use some of the prepackaged cooked bacon. I find that the ones labeled "thick cut" taste best.

COLLARD GREENS

Makes 4 servings

Ingredients:

1 bunch fresh collard greens

½ cup smoked ham, diced

1 cup chicken stock

½ teaspoon chili flakes

½ teaspoon apple cider vinegar

Kosher salt and fresh pepper to taste

Method:

1. *Wash collard greens very well in cold water, removing any sand.*

2. *Tear stems away by folding each leaf in half then pulling the stem away (if you prefer, leave the stems on and cut each leaf into wide strips).*

3. *Divide the collard greens between the 3 steamer baskets.*

4. *Fill water tank with water.*

5. *Cover steamer and set timer to 30 minutes.*

6. *Steam for 10 minutes for just done collard greens or up to 30 minutes if desired.*

7. *While greens are steaming, combine remaining ingredients in a microwave-safe bowl.*

8. *Microwave for 2-3 minutes or until hot then set aside.*

9. *When steaming is complete, divide the collard greens between bowls.*

10. *Pour ham mixture over the collard greens, stir it in and garnish as desired before serving.*

TIP

Serve this dish with cornbread. I love sopping up the delicious broth with it.

MAPLE GLAZED CARROTS

Makes 4 servings

Ingredients:

1 pound carrots, peeled

2 tablespoons unsalted butter

⅓ cup maple syrup

½ teaspoon kosher salt

2 tablespoons chicken stock

1 teaspoon fresh parsley, chopped

Method:

1. *Cut carrots ½-inch thick on the bias.*
2. *Fill water tank with water.*
3. *Place the carrots in steamer basket(s).*
4. *Cover steamer and set timer to 14 minutes.*
5. *Steam for 14 minutes or until fork tender.*
6. *While steaming, combine remaining ingredients, except parsley, in a large saucepan over medium-high heat.*
7. *Boil for 5 minutes or until mixture is thick and syrup-like.*
8. *When steaming is complete, transfer the carrots to the syrup mixture.*
9. *Stir gently to coat the carrots.*
10. *Pour into a serving bowl, sprinkle with parsley and serve.*

TIP
You can use this same recipe and substitute parsnips for the carrots.

MARINATED BELL PEPPERS

Makes 3 servings

Ingredients:

2 red bell peppers, halved, cored and seeded

2 yellow bell peppers, halved, cored and seeded

1 tablespoon balsamic vinegar

¼ cup olive oil

4 fresh basil leaves, chopped

¼ teaspoon dried thyme

Kosher salt and fresh pepper to taste

Method:

1. *Fill water tank with water.*
2. *Arrange the bell pepper halves in the middle steamer basket.*
3. *Cover steamer and set timer to 30 minutes.*
4. *Steam for 25-30 minutes or until tender.*
5. *While steaming, combine remaining ingredients in a small bowl; whisk to combine.*
6. *When steaming is complete, remove peppers from the steamer basket; let cool.*
7. *Peel off the skin from the peppers then cut into 1-inch strips.*
8. *Transfer the strips to a shallow baking dish.*
9. *Pour vinegar mixture over the peppers; toss to coat.*
10. *Cover and refrigerate overnight before serving cold.*

GREEN BEANS
WITH LEMON

Makes 4 servings

Ingredients:

1¼ pounds fresh green beans

1 tablespoon olive oil

1 tablespoon fresh lemon juice

Kosher salt and fresh pepper to taste

Lemon slices

Method:

1. *Fill water tank with water.*
2. *Place green beans in the top steamer basket.*
3. *Cover steamer and set timer to 15 minutes.*
4. *Steam for 12-15 minutes or until green beans are bright green and tender.*
5. *Remove steaming basket and drain on a towel.*
6. *Transfer the green beans to a serving bowl.*
7. *Toss with remaining ingredients and serve warm.*

TIP
Try this recipe using lime or tangerine.
It is equally delicious but
a completely different taste.

SPICY CORN ON THE COB

Makes 4 servings

Ingredients:

4-6 ears of fresh corn

3 tablespoons unsalted butter

1 tablespoon cayenne pepper

Kosher salt to taste

Method:

1. *Fill water tank with water.*

2. *Place corn in the bottom and middle steamer baskets.*

3. *Cover steamer and set timer to 6 minutes.*

4. *Steam for 5-6 minutes or until corn is tender.*

5. *Place butter and cayenne pepper in a heat-proof ramekin then place it in the top steamer basket during the last 3 minutes of steaming.*

6. *When steaming is complete, remove corn using tongs.*

7. *Brush with melted butter, season with salt and serve.*

TIP

This recipe was inspired by Mexican street corn. To be truly authentic, use mayonnaise instead of the melted butter.

BUTTERNUT SQUASH SOUP

Makes 4 servings

Ingredients:

2 small butternut squash, cut in half

4 teaspoons unsalted butter, melted

4 tablespoons brown sugar

Pinch of kosher salt

Pinch of fresh pepper

4 cups chicken stock

1 cup half & half or whole milk

1 tablespoon honey

1 teaspoon fresh ginger, chopped

2 teaspoons apple cider vinegar

Sour cream and fresh parsley for garnish (optional)

Method:

1. *Fill water tank with water.*

2. *Place the squash in steamer basket(s).*

3. *Top each squash half with butter, sugar, salt and pepper.*

4. *Cover steamer and set timer to 20 minutes.*

5. *Steam for 18-20 minutes or until fork tender.*

6. *In a stockpot, combine the chicken stock, half & half, honey, ginger, and vinegar; bring to a simmer.*

7. *Let squash cool for 5 minutes then remove the seeds and peel from the squash.*

8. *Add the squash to the stockpot.*

9. *Purée using an immersion blender until smooth.*

10. *Ladle into bowls, garnish with sour cream and parsley if desired and serve.*

TIP

Instead of the brown sugar, you can also use a sweetener such as Zsweet.

LEEK & POTATO SOUP

Makes 6 servings

Ingredients:

6 cups Russet potatoes, peeled, rinsed and cubed

6 cups leeks, rinsed and chopped

2 tablespoons unsalted butter, melted

6 cups chicken stock, heated

1 teaspoon kosher salt

½ teaspoon fresh pepper

1 tablespoon fresh lemon juice

2 teaspoons honey

1 teaspoon crushed red pepper flakes

½ cup heavy cream

Method:

1. *Fill water tank with water.*

2. *Place the potatoes in the bottom steamer basket.*

3. *Place the leeks in the middle steamer basket; set aside.*

4. *Fit steamer with potato basket only, cover and set timer to 20 minutes.*

5. *Steam the potatoes for 10 minutes.*

6. *After potatoes have steamed for 10 minutes, carefully add the leek steamer basket above the potatoes and continue steaming for the remaining 10 minutes.*

7. *In a stockpot over medium-high, combine the remaining ingredients; bring to a simmer.*

8. *When steaming is complete, transfer the potatoes and leeks to the stockpot.*

9. *Use an immersion blender to purée the ingredients until smooth.*

10. *Garnish as desired and serve.*

EDAMAME SOUP

Makes 4 servings

Ingredients:

1 pound Edamame, shelled

½ small yellow onion, separated

2½ cups chicken stock

1⅔ cups milk

1½ tablespoons unsalted butter

1 teaspoon fresh ginger, chopped

Kosher salt and fresh pepper to taste

Method:

1. *Fill water tank with water.*
2. *Place the Edamame and onions in separate steamer baskets.*
3. *Cover steamer and set timer to 5 minutes.*
4. *Steam for 4-5 minutes or until tender.*
5. *In a stockpot, combine remaining ingredients; bring to a simmer over medium heat.*
6. *When steaming is complete, remove steamer baskets and place on a towel to drain.*
7. *Transfer the Edamame and onions to the stockpot.*
8. *Use an immersion blender to purée the ingredients until smooth.*
9. *Taste and adjust seasoning if desired.*
10. *Ladle into bowls and serve.*

MIXED VEGGIE
SALAD

Makes 4 servings

Ingredients:

2 fresh beets, quartered

1 small head cauliflower, cut into florets

½ pound fresh green beans cut into 2-inch lengths

2 tablespoons red wine vinegar

2 tablespoons red onion, minced

1 tablespoon Dijon mustard

Kosher salt and fresh pepper to taste

½ cup extra-virgin olive oil

1 cup fresh button mushrooms, thinly sliced

½ cup goat cheese, crumbled

Method:

1. *Line the bottom steamer basket with parchment paper then place the beets in the basket(s) (the parchment will help prevent staining).*

2. *Fill water tank with water.*

3. *Cover steamer and set timer to 20 minutes.*

4. *When steaming is complete, test if beets are fork tender, usually they need a few more minutes. At this time place the cauliflower in the middle steamer basket, green beans in the top steamer basket and keep the beets in the bottom steamer basket.*

5. *Cover steamer and set timer to 5 minutes.*

6. *Steam for 5 minutes or until the cauliflower and green beans are crisp-tender.*

7. *Remove and let vegetables cool slightly.*

8. *In a large bowl whisk together the remaining ingredients, except mushrooms and goat cheese.*

9. *Peel the skins off of the beets (use gloves if desired) and slice them thinly.*

10. *Toss all of the cooked vegetables in the vinaigrette in the bowl; coat evenly.*

11. *Add the mushrooms and cheese then toss gently to mix without breaking up the mushrooms.*

12. *Serve warm or cold.*

COPPER PENNIES
SALAD
Makes 6 servings

Ingredients:

2 pounds large carrots, peeled

½ cup apple cider vinegar

¼ cup canola oil

½ cup granulated sugar

2 teaspoons dry mustard

1 teaspoon Worcestershire sauce

1 can (10¾ ounces) condensed tomato soup

Kosher salt and fresh pepper to taste

1 small red onion, sliced very thinly into rings

1 green bell pepper, sliced

Method:

1. *Fill water tank with water.*

2. *Divide the carrots between the steamer baskets, cutting them to fit if necessary.*

3. *Cover steamer and set timer to 15 minutes.*

4. *When steaming is complete, test for tenderness using a paring knife.*

5. *Remove and let cool slightly.*

6. *Cut the carrots into very thin coins using a knife, slicing blade of a food processor or a mandoline.*

7. *In a large serving bowl, whisk together the vinegar, oil, sugar, mustard, Worcestershire sauce, tomato soup, salt and pepper.*

8. *Add the carrots, onions and bell peppers to the bowl and stir thoroughly.*

9. *Taste and adjust salt if desired.*

10. *Cover and refrigerate for a minimum of 6 hours before serving.*

STUFFED MUSHROOMS

Makes 12 mushrooms

Ingredients:

¼ cup Italian-style breadcrumbs

¼ cup Parmesan cheese, grated

1 garlic clove, peeled and minced

⅛ cup red bell peppers, finely diced

1 tablespoon olive oil

Kosher salt and fresh pepper to taste

12 large button mushrooms (2½-inch in diameter), stemmed

2 tablespoons fresh parsley, chopped

Method:

1. *In a bowl, combine the breadcrumbs, cheese, garlic, bell peppers, oil, salt and pepper.*

2. *Spoon mixture into the mushroom caps (pack the mixture down).*

3. *Fill water tank with water.*

4. *Place the mushrooms in steamer basket(s).*

5. *Cover steamer and set timer to 10 minutes.*

6. *Steam for 8-10 minutes or until mushrooms are darkened in color and filling is hot all the way through.*

7. *When steaming is complete, remove from steamer.*

8. *Garnish with parsley and serve immediately.*

TIP

If you have little bits of leftover vegetables in your refrigerator, chop them up and add them to this recipe. Corn, peas, green bans or spinach work great, just don't add more than 1/3 cup of chopped vegetables or the taste gets too watered down.

CILANTRO RICE

Makes 4 servings

Ingredients:

2 cups basmati rice, rinsed

1 tablespoon unsalted butter

Boiling water

1 teaspoon lime zest

½ cup cilantro, chopped

Kosher salt to taste

Method:

1. *Place the rice tray in bottom steamer basket.*
2. *Place the rice in the rice tray.*
3. *Pour enough boiling water over the rice until ½-inch above the rice.*
4. *Add the butter and stir.*
5. *Fill water tank with water.*
6. *Cover steamer and set timer to 30 minutes.*
7. *Steam for 30 minutes or until rice is tender.*
8. *In a bowl, combine remaining ingredients, except salt.*
9. *When steaming is complete, pour rice into the bowl.*
10. *Stir to combine then season with salt.*
11. *Serve immediately.*

COCONUT RICE

Makes 4 servings

Ingredients:

2 cups basmati rice, rinsed

½ cup coconut milk

Boiling water

¼ cup coconut flakes

2 green onions, chopped

Method:

1. *Place the rice tray in bottom steamer basket.*

2. *Place the rice in the rice tray.*

3. *Pour coconut milk and enough boiling water over the rice until ½-inch above the rice.*

4. *Fill water tank with water.*

5. *Cover steamer and set timer to 30 minutes.*

6. *Steam for 30 minutes or until rice is tender.*

7. *When steaming is complete, pour the rice into a serving dish and fluff using a fork.*

8. *Garnish with coconut flakes and green onions before serving.*

TIP

To make this recipe using brown rice, simply increase the water by 1/3 cup and steam for an additional 15-20 minutes.

COUSCOUS PILAF

Makes 4 servings

Ingredients:

2 cups Israeli couscous

1 tablespoon powdered chicken bouillon

2 cups boiling water

1 green onion, chopped

1 garlic clove, chopped

¼ cup almonds, sliced

¼ cup raisins

¼ cup apricots, diced

1 teaspoon crushed red pepper

1 teaspoon vinegar

2-4 tablespoons olive oil

Method:

1. *Fill water tank with water.*
2. *Pour couscous in the rice tray then place it in the bottom steamer basket.*
3. *In a bowl, stir the chicken bouillon into the boiling water then pour over couscous.*
4. *Cover steamer and set timer to 10 minutes.*
5. *Steam for 10 minutes or until couscous is tender.*
6. *In a mixing bowl, combine remaining ingredients.*
7. *When steaming is complete, transfer couscous to the mixing bowl and stir gently.*
8. *Taste and adjust seasoning if desired.*
9. *Garnish as desired and serve immediately.*

DEVILED EGGS

Makes 6 servings

Ingredients:

12 large eggs

½ cup mayonnaise

2 teaspoons yellow mustard

2 tablespoons sweet pickle relish

1 teaspoon kosher salt

½ teaspoon granulated sugar

⅛ teaspoon cayenne pepper

2 teaspoons cider vinegar

Paprika for sprinkling

Method:

1. *Fill water tank with water.*

2. *Place eggs in steamer basket(s).*

3. *Cover steamer and set timer to 10 minutes.*

4. *When steaming is complete, remove basket(s) and place on a towel to drain.*

5. *Let rest for 5 minutes.*

6. *Crack each egg multiple times against the side of the kitchen sink then peel the eggs under a hard stream of cold water from the faucet.*

7. *Cut the eggs in half lengthwise, remove the egg yolks then place the yolks into a mixing bowl.*

8. *Mash the egg yolks using a fork.*

9. *Rinse the egg white halves, wrap them in plastic wrap and chill until ready to use.*

10. *Add remaining ingredients, except paprika, to the egg yolks; mix well using a large spoon then taste to adjust seasoning if desired.*

11. *Transfer the egg mixture to a pastry bag and pipe into the egg white halves.*

12. *Sprinkle with paprika then cover and chill until ready to serve.*

VEGGIES & SIDES

EGG SALAD

Makes 4 servings

Ingredients:

12 large eggs

½ cup mayonnaise

2 teaspoons yellow mustard

2 tablespoons sweet pickle relish

¼ medium yellow onion, finely chopped

1 teaspoon kosher salt

½ teaspoon granulated sugar

⅛ teaspoon cayenne pepper

2 teaspoons cider vinegar

Method:

1. *Fill water tank with water.*
2. *Place the eggs in steamer basket(s).*
3. *Cover steamer and set timer to 10 minutes.*
4. *In a mixing bowl, combine remaining ingredients; set aside.*
5. *When steaming is complete, remove steamer basket(s) and place on a towel to drain.*
6. *Let rest for 5 minutes.*
7. *Crack each egg multiple times against the side of the kitchen sink.*
8. *Peel the eggs under a hard stream of cold water from the faucet.*
9. *Chop the eggs into small to medium pieces using a knife, fork or potato masher.*
10. *Add the eggs to the mixing bowl; stir to combine.*
11. *Taste to adjust seasoning if desired and serve.*

TIP
Use this egg salad
to make a wonderful
sandwich.

GERMAN POTATO SALAD

Makes 4-6 servings

Ingredients:

3 pounds petite red bliss potatoes

¼ cup apple cider vinegar

2 teaspoons dry mustard

1 tablespoon canola oil

¼ cup chicken stock

2 tablespoons granulated sugar or sugar substitute

½ medium red onion, diced

3 bacon slices, cooked and crumbled

2 tablespoons fresh parsley, chopped

Kosher salt and fresh pepper to taste

Method:

1. *Fill water tank with water.*
2. *Divide the potatoes between the 3 steamer baskets.*
3. *Cover steamer and set timer to 18 minutes.*
4. *Steam for 18 minutes or until potatoes are just below fork tender.*
5. *While steaming, combine remaining ingredients in a microwave-safe glass bowl.*
6. *Microwave for 2-3 minutes or until hot then remove and set aside.*
7. *When steaming is complete, slice the hot potatoes into a large bowl.*
8. *Pour the hot vinegar mixture over the potatoes and stir to coat.*
9. *Taste and adjust seasoning if desired and serve warm or cold.*

TIP

Since this salad does not contain mayonnaise or eggs, it is a great one to prepare for a buffet, a pot luck, picnic or any occasion where food is left without refrigeration for a longer period of time.

RED BLISS MASHED POTATOES

Makes 4-6 servings

Ingredients:

3 pounds petite red bliss potatoes, skin on

3 tablespoons unsalted butter

Kosher salt to taste

1 cup whole milk or half & half

Method:

1. *Select potatoes that are similar in size, halving any that are too large.*
2. *Fill water tank with water.*
3. *Divide potatoes between the 3 steamer baskets.*
4. *Cover steamer and set timer to 20 minutes.*
5. *Steam for 20 minutes or until potatoes are fork tender.*
6. *When steaming is complete, transfer potatoes to a bowl suitable for mashing.*
7. *Add the butter and a bit of salt to the bowl; mash using a potato masher.*
8. *Add the milk in stages until desired texture is reached (add more milk if needed).*
9. *Taste and adjust salt if desired and serve immediately.*

TIP

Some of my favorite add-ins to mashed potatoes are goat cheese, pesto or store-bought tapenade. For a healthier version, use a little olive oil and buttermilk instead of milk.

SWEET POTATO
PUREE

Makes 4 servings

Ingredients:

2 pounds sweet potatoes, peeled and cut into 1-inch chunks

4 tablespoons unsalted butter

6 ginger snap cookies

2 tablespoons granulated sugar

2 teaspoons fresh lemon juice

½ cup heavy cream or whole milk

Kosher salt and fresh pepper taste

Method:

1. *Fill water tank with water.*
2. *Place the potatoes in steamer basket(s).*
3. *Cover steamer and set timer to 20 minutes.*
4. *Steam for 20 minutes or until tender.*
5. *Place remaining ingredients in a food processor.*
6. *When steaming is complete, transfer the potatoes to the food processor.*
7. *Pulse until smooth (process in batches if needed).*
8. *Taste and adjust seasoning if desired before serving.*

TIP

For a different taste, try adding some star anise or ginger (or both) to this puree.

GOOEY STEAMED
SWEET POTATOES

Makes 4 servings

Ingredients:

2 large sweet potatoes, sliced in half lengthwise

4 teaspoons unsalted butter

Kosher salt to taste

Ground cinnamon, for sprinkling

4 teaspoons maple syrup

1 cup mini marshmallows

Method:

1. *Arrange the potatoes in steamer basket(s).*

2. *Fill water tank with water.*

3. *Cover steamer and set timer to 18 minutes.*

4. *Steam for 18 minutes or until potatoes are fork tender.*

5. *When steaming is complete, remove steamer basket(s) and poke holes all over the cut surface using a fork.*

6. *Spread a teaspoon of butter over each potato then season with salt.*

7. *Sprinkle with cinnamon and drizzle with maple syrup.*

8. *Top each potato with marshmallows then return to the steamer.*

9. *Steam for an additional 1-2 minutes or just until marshmallows begin to melt.*

10. *Remove potatoes using a spatula and serve immediately.*

TIP

For a nice crunch, add a layer of chopped pecans under the marshmallows.

HERBED POTATOES

Makes 4 servings

Ingredients:

1½ pounds small red potatoes

2 tablespoons unsalted butter, melted

1 teaspoon fresh thyme, chopped

1 teaspoon fresh oregano, chopped

1 teaspoon fresh parsley, chopped

Kosher salt and fresh pepper to taste

Method:

1. *Fill water tank with water.*
2. *Arrange the potatoes in the top steamer basket.*
3. *Cover steamer and set timer to 30 minutes.*
4. *Steam for 25-30 minutes or until potatoes are tender.*
5. *When steaming is complete, remove steaming basket and drain on a towel.*
6. *Transfer the potatoes to a serving bowl.*
7. *Toss with remaining ingredients and serve warm.*

SILKY CAULIFLOWER PUREE

Makes 4 servings

Ingredients:

1 large head cauliflower, cut into florets

1 cup chicken stock

½ cup whole milk

1 tablespoon unsalted butter

Kosher salt and fresh pepper to taste

Method:

1. *Fill water tank with water.*

2. *Place the cauliflower in steamer basket(s).*

3. *Cover steamer and set timer to 7 minutes.*

4. *Steam for 7 minutes or until cauliflower are just tender.*

5. *When steaming is complete, transfer cauliflower to a food processor or blender.*

6. *Add remaining ingredients to the food processor or blender.*

7. *Purée mixture until very smooth.*

8. *Add a little more milk if the texture is too thick for your liking.*

9. *Taste and adjust seasoning before serving.*

TIP

To make this a pesto-flavored cauliflower purée without adding lots of calories, add 3 garlic cloves and a handful of fresh basil leaves to the food processor before pureeing.

RIGATONI WITH BROCCOLI

Makes 2 servings

Ingredients:

3 cups broccoli florets

½ pound Rigatoni pasta, cooked

1 tablespoon butter, melted

3 garlic cloves, chopped

Fresh pepper to taste

¼ cup Parmesan cheese, grated (optional)

Method:

1. *Fill water tank with water.*
2. *Place the broccoli in the middle steamer basket.*
3. *Cover steamer and set timer to 6 minutes.*
4. *Steam for 5-6 minutes or until broccoli are bright green but still crisp.*
5. *While steaming, combine remaining ingredients, except cheese, in a mixing bowl.*
6. *When steaming is complete, remove steaming basket and place on a towel to drain.*
7. *Transfer the broccoli to the mixing bowl; add the cheese then toss to combine.*
8. *Serve immediately.*

TIP

If you don't eat pasta, try substituting with rice noodles. They soften so easily, you can just add them to the steamer with the broccoli and skip boiling them in water.

BUTTERMILK
CUSTARD CUPS

Makes 6 servings

Ingredients:

1 cup granulated sugar

⅔ cup light brown sugar, packed

½ cup unsalted butter, melted

1 teaspoon pure vanilla extract

¼ cup buttermilk

⅔ cup heavy cream

8 large egg yolks

Method:

1. *Fill water tank with water.*

2. *Apply nonstick spray to six 4-ounce ramekins.*

3. *Place the ramekins in steamer basket(s).*

4. *In a blender, combine all ingredients; cover with lid.*

5. *Pulse blender until mixture is smooth and frothy.*

6. *Pour mixture into prepared ramekins then cover each with aluminum foil.*

7. *Cover steamer and set timer to 18 minutes.*

8. *When steaming is complete, carefully remove a ramekin and check for doneness, it should be a bit wobbly (steam for an additional 2 minutes if not done).*

9. *Carefully remove custards and chill for 1 hour before serving.*

TIP

Try adding some chocolate pieces and/or raspberries to the bottom of each ramekin before pouring in the custard.

CRÈME BRÛLÉE

Makes 6 servings

Ingredients:

2 cups heavy cream

1 vanilla bean, split (see source page 140)

½ cup granulated sugar + more for burning tops

7 large egg yolks

Method:

1. *Combine the heavy cream and vanilla bean in a saucepan over medium heat.*
2. *Bring to a simmer until bubbles form around the edges of the pan; remove from heat.*
3. *Let rest for 10 minutes.*
4. *In a bowl, whisk together the sugar and egg yolks until very smooth.*
5. *Strain cream mixture into the sugar mixture; whisk to combine.*
6. *Place six 4-ounce ramekins inside the steamer basket(s).*
7. *Divide mixture between the ramekins, filling ramekins almost to the top.*
8. *Carefully cover each ramekins with a small square of aluminum foil.*
9. *Fill water tank with water.*
10. *Cover steamer and set timer to 12 minutes.*
11. *Steam for 10-12 minutes then check for doneness (custards should be wobbly).*
12. *Remove and chill for a minimum of 1 hour.*
13. *To serve, remove crème brûlée and place on a cookie sheet.*
14. *Sprinkle the top of each dessert with a thin, even layer of sugar.*
15. *Use a blow torch (see source page 140) to caramelize the sugar.*
16. *Sprinkle with a second even layer of sugar then blow torch to caramelize again.*
17. *Let rest for 5 minutes to let the sugar cool before eating.*

DESSERTS

JUICY STEAMED PEACHES

Makes 4 servings

DESSERTS

Ingredients:

2 medium peaches, cut in half and seeds removed

½ cup peach nectar

4 teaspoons granulated sugar

Method:

1. *Place 1 peach half into each of 4 ramekins.*
2. *Pour 2 tablespoons of peach nectar over each peach half.*
3. *Sprinkle sugar over each peach half then cover ramekins tightly with aluminum foil.*
4. *Fill water tank with water.*
5. *Place ramekins in steamer basket(s) (if using two steamer baskets, the one on top will need about 2-3 additional minutes of steaming time).*
6. *Cover steamer and set timer to 7 minutes.*
7. *Steam for 5-7 minutes or until fork tender.*
8. *When steaming is complete, remove from steamer, garnish as desired and serve.*

TIP

For a grown up version, substitute the peach nectar with peach-flavored liqueur.

STEAMED DESSERT
PEARS

Makes 4 servings

Ingredients:

4 Bosc pears

1 teaspoon fresh lemon juice

2 tablespoons granulated sugar or sweetener

2 tablespoons pear-flavored jelly beans (optional)

3 tablespoons pecans, toasted and chopped

Method:

1. *Lay pears on their sides and trim a small slice from the bottom so they will sit flat.*
2. *Remove the seeds from the thickest part of the pear using a melon baller.*
3. *Use the melon baller to remove the core and seeds but do not pierce the bottom.*
4. *In a small bowl, stir together remaining ingredients.*
5. *Fill each pear cavity with the pecan mixture.*
6. *Fill water tank with water.*
7. *Place the pears in steamer basket(s).*
8. *Cover steamer and set timer to 15 minutes.*
9. *Steam for 15 minutes or until pears are fork tender.*
10. *When steaming is complete, remove carefully, making sure not to spill out the now liquid center.*
11. *Serve warm.*

TIP

For a lovely sauce to serve with these pears, dissolve more of the pear-flavored jelly beans in a bit of water in the microwave. You can add a bit of pear-flavored brandy to the sauce as well.

MANDARIN ORANGE
PUDDING CAKES

Makes 6 servings

Ingredients:

¼ cup all purpose flour

¾ cup granulated sugar, divided

1 cup milk

3 large eggs, separated

Zest of 2 Mandarin oranges or tangerines

¼ cup fresh Mandarin orange or tangerine juice

1 tablespoon fresh lemon juice

½ teaspoon vanilla extract

¼ cup unsalted butter, melted

¼ teaspoon kosher salt

Method:

1. *Lightly apply nonstick cooking spray to 6 individual custard cups.*

2. *In a large bowl, sift together the flour and ½ cup of sugar.*

3. *In a separate mixing bowl, whisk together the milk and egg yolks.*

4. *Whisk the zest, juices, vanilla and butter into the milk mixture.*

5. *Add the flour mixture and salt; whisk until combined then set aside.*

6. *In a completely clean and dry bowl, whisk the egg whites rapidly using a clean whisk.*

7. *While whisking, sprinkle in remaining ¼ cup of sugar; whisk for 1 minute or until soft peaks form.*

8. *Pour egg whites over top of the milk mixture; fold in until combined without deflating.*

9. *Ladle batter into the custard cups, filling them almost to the top (reach to the bottom of the bowl as you pick up the ladle to get both the runnier liquid at the bottom and the foamier liquid on top).*

10. *Cover tops with a piece of aluminum foil then fill water tank with water.*

11. *Carefully place the ramekins in steamer basket(s).*

12. *Cover steamer and set timer to 18 minutes.*

13. *Steam for 18 minutes or until cakes are slightly wobbly in the center.*

14. *Remove and let stand until warm.*

15. *To serve run a thin paring knife around the sides of each ramekin.*

16. *Invert onto a serving plate and serve.*

MINI STRAWBERRY
CHEESECAKES

Makes 6 servings

Ingredients:

6 vanilla wafer cookies

6 large strawberries, stemmed

1 package (8 ounces) cream cheese, softened

4 tablespoons granulated sugar

4 large egg yolks

1 large egg

Fresh berries, for serving

Method:

1. *Apply nonstick spray to six 4–ounce ramekins or silicone baking cups.*
2. *Drop a vanilla wafer into the bottom of each ramekin, flat-side down; set aside.*
3. *In a food processor, combine the strawberries, cream cheese and sugar.*
4. *Purée until smooth then add remaining ingredients, except berries for serving, and pulse just to combine.*
5. *Divide mixture evenly over the top of each wafer, filling ramekins almost to the top.*
6. *Cover each ramekin with a small square of nonstick aluminum foil.*
7. *Fill water tank with water.*
8. *Arrange the ramekins in steamer basket(s).*
9. *Cover steamer and set timer to 18 minutes.*
10. *Steam for 18 minutes or until centers are just wobbly; remove immediately.*
11. *Chill for several hours before removing the foil.*
12. *Garnish with additional berries before serving.*

MINI CHOCOLATE CAKES

Makes 4 servings

Ingredients:

1 cup good quality cocoa powder (see source page 140)

2 cups unbleached all purpose flour

1 teaspoon baking powder

½ teaspoon baking soda

1 teaspoon kosher salt

¾ cup unsalted butter, softened

2 cups granulated sugar

3 large eggs

2 teaspoons vanilla extract

1½ cups whole milk

Method:

1. *Apply nonstick spray to four 4-ounce ramekins or silicone molds; set aside.*
2. *In a bowl, whisk together the cocoa, flour, baking powder baking soda and salt; set aside.*
3. *In a separate bowl, cream together the butter and sugar using a hand or stand mixer until fluffy.*
4. *Add the eggs and vanilla; beat until smooth then scrape the bowl.*
5. *Add the milk and flour mixture; mix until smooth.*
6. *Pour batter into ramekins, filling each 2/3 full (reserve extra batter for later use).*
7. *Cover each ramekin with a small square of nonstick aluminum foil.*
8. *Fill water tank with water.*
9. *Place the ramekins in steamer basket(s).*
10. *Cover steamer and set timer to 12 minutes.*
11. *Steam for 12 minutes or until cakes are just wobbly in the center.*
12. *When steaming is complete, serve warm with desired garnishes.*

TIP

Extra batter keeps well, covered and refrigerated for up to 1 week. Enjoy fresh, warm cakes as desired instead of steaming a larger batch and reheating them later.

DESSERTS

MORNING GLORY
MUFFINS

Makes 8 muffins

Ingredients:

2 large eggs

⅓ cup canola oil

1 teaspoon vanilla extract

½ cup light brown sugar

1 cup all purpose flour

1 teaspoon baking soda

1 teaspoon ground allspice

½ teaspoon kosher salt

½ cup dark raisins

1 cup carrots, grated

1 cup apples

½ cup coconut flakes

½ cup pecans, chopped

Method:

1. *Apply nonstick spray to eight 4-ounce ramekins or silicone muffin cups; set aside.*

2. *In a large bowl, whisk together eggs, oil, vanilla and sugar.*

3. *In a separate bowl, whisk together flour, baking soda, allspice and salt.*

4. *Add remaining ingredients to the egg mixture then fold in the flour mixture until just combined.*

5. *Spoon batter into prepared ramekins until 2/3 full.*

6. *Cover each ramekin with a small square of aluminum foil.*

7. *Fill water tank with water.*

8. *Arrange the ramekins in steamer basket(s).*

9. *Cover steamer and set timer to 15 minutes.*

10. *When steaming is complete, test for doneness by inserting a bamboo skewer off-center, it should come out with just a few moist crumbs clinging to it. If the skewer has a streak of shiny batter, continue steaming for an additional 2-3 minutes.*

11. *When muffins are done, serve warm or at room temperature.*

PINEAPPLE TAPIOCA
PUDDING

Makes 6 servings

Ingredients:

1 bag (4 ounces) large pearl tapioca, soaked for 2 hours then drained

3 cups boiling whole milk

½ cup cream of coconut

½ teaspoon kosher salt

1 cup granulated sugar or other sweetener

1 teaspoon vanilla extract

2 teaspoons fresh lemon juice

1 cup fresh pineapple, diced small + more for serving

Method:

1. *Place the drained tapioca and boiling milk into the rice tray.*

2. *Fill water tank with water.*

3. *Place rice tray in the bottom steamer basket.*

4. *Cover steamer and set timer to 30 minutes.*

5. *When steaming is complete, remove and add remaining ingredients; stir well.*

6. *Place in the steamer again and set timer for 8 minutes.*

7. *When steaming is complete, carefully remove and stir (if mixture seems too thick, add some more milk).*

8. *Let cool slightly then serve with a pineapple spear.*

TIP
Any refrigerated tapioca will thicken considerably. If you want it to soften, warm it then add a little bit more milk.

RICE
PUDDING

Makes 4 servings

Ingredients:

½ cup granulated sugar

1½ cups milk

½ cup heavy cream

1 teaspoon vanilla extract

1 teaspoon ground cinnamon

Pinch of kosher salt

2 cups rice, cooked

DESSERTS

Method:

1. *In a large bowl, combine all ingredients.*
2. *Spoon mixture into ramekins.*
3. *Cover each ramekin with a small square of aluminum foil.*
4. *Fill water tank with water.*
5. *Place ramekins in steamer basket(s) (if using two steamer baskets, the one on top will need about 2-3 minutes of additional steaming time).*
6. *Cover steamer and set timer to 15 minutes.*
7. *Steam for 13-15 minutes or until set.*
8. *Remove from steamer, garnish as desired and serve.*

TIP
Add some dried fruit
to the rice pudding
if desired.

116

STEAM-BAKED APPLES
WITH CINNAMON

Makes 4 servings

Ingredients:

4 baking apples

2 tablespoons dark raisins

4 tablespoons granulated sugar or other sweetener

2 teaspoons ground cinnamon

A small pinch of kosher salt

1 teaspoon vanilla extract

Method:

1. *Use a melon baller to remove stems and seeds from each apple, being careful not to make a hole in the bottom of each apple (a melon baller is much better for this task than an apple corer).*

2. *In a small bowl, stir together remaining ingredients.*

3. *Fill the hollowed out space in each apple with the raisin mixture.*

4. *Arrange the apples in steamer basket(s).*

5. *Fill water tank with water.*

6. *Cover steamer and set timer to 18 minutes.*

7. *Steam for 18 minutes then use a fork to test for tenderness.*

8. *When steaming is complete, remove carefully trying not to tip out any of the now liquid center.*

9. *Serve hot or warm.*

TIP
Pink Lady apples are nice for this recipe too. You can add a few red hot cinnamon candies to the center of each apple for a nice twist.

STEAMED CRANBERRY
DESSERT CAKES

Makes 6 servings

Ingredients:

⅓ cup unsalted butter, softened

1 cup granulated sugar

2 large eggs, beaten

2 cups all purpose flour

½ teaspoon kosher salt or ¼ teaspoon other salt

2½ teaspoons baking powder

⅓ cup whole milk

1 teaspoon fresh orange zest

1½ cups fresh or frozen cranberries

½ cup walnuts or pecans, toasted and chopped

Whipped cream, for serving (optional)

Method:

1. *Apply nonstick spray to six 4-ounce ramekins; set aside.*
2. *In a large mixing bowl, cream the butter using a wooden spoon.*
3. *Add the sugar and mix until smooth then add the eggs.*
4. *Stir in the flour, salt and baking powder; mix well.*
5. *Add remaining ingredients, except whipped cream; mix until smooth.*
6. *Divide mixture between the ramekins then cover each with aluminum foil.*
7. *Fill water tank with water.*
8. *Place the ramekins in steamer basket(s).*
9. *Cover steamer and set timer to 20 minutes.*
10. *When steaming is complete, carefully remove one ramekin, take off the foil and test the center for doneness using a paring knife, it should come out clean. If not done, steam for an additional 3-4 more minutes.*
11. *When steaming is complete, carefully remove and let cool slightly.*
12. *Remove foils and serve with whipped cream if desired.*

RHUBARB
CRUNCH

Makes 4 servings

Ingredients:

3 cups fresh or frozen rhubarb, sliced

⅔ cup granulated sugar or other sweetener, divided

3 white bread slices, crusts removed and diced

2 tablespoons unsalted butter, melted

Method:

1. *In a bowl, toss together the rhubarb and half of the sugar.*

2. *Divide the rhubarb mixture between 4 ramekins, piling it high.*

3. *Cover each ramekin with a piece of aluminum foil.*

4. *Fill water tank with water.*

5. *Place the ramekins in steamer basket(s).*

6. *Cover steamer and set timer to 18 minutes.*

7. *When steaming is complete, carefully remove and set aside.*

8. *Preheat oven to 350°F.*

9. *In a small bowl, toss together the bread cubes, butter and remaining sugar.*

10. *Spread bread mixture out on a cookie sheet.*

11. *Bake for 15 minutes or until golden brown.*

12. *Remove foil from the ramekins and top with crispy bread cubes before serving.*

TIP

For a cinnamon-toast taste, add a bit of ground cinnamon to the bread cube topping. The taste is irresistible.

BLUEBERRY CREAM
CHEESE MINIS

Makes 6 servings

Ingredients:

½ cup blueberries

4 ounces cream cheese, softened

3 tablespoons granulated sugar

1⅓ cups half & half

4 large egg yolks

1 large egg

More fresh berries, for serving

Method:

1. *In a blender combine the blueberries, cream cheese and sugar.*

2. *Purée until smooth.*

3. *Add remaining ingredients, except berries for serving, and purée for 5 seconds.*

4. *Apply nonstick spray to 6 small decorative molds or ramekins.*

5. *Divide mixture between the molds.*

6. *Cover each mold with a piece of aluminum foil.*

7. *Fill water tank with water.*

8. *Place the ramekins in steamer basket(s).*

9. *Cover steamer and set timer to 15 minutes.*

10. *Steaming is done when centers are just wobbly (add 2-3 minutes of steaming time if needed).*

11. *Remove immediately.*

12. *Chill for several hours before removing foil and inverting onto a serving dish.*

13. *Garnish with additional berries before serving.*

CARAMEL
BANANA CRUNCH

Makes 4 servings

Ingredients:

4 bananas

½ of a lemon, for squeezing

4 tablespoons jarred caramel sauce

Small pinch of kosher salt

½ teaspoon vanilla extract

1 tablespoon banana liqueur (optional)

4 teaspoons unsalted butter, melted

4 tablespoons macadamia nuts, toasted and chopped

Method:

1. *Slice the bananas into 4 individual ramekins.*
2. *Squeeze a little bit of lemon juice over the bananas in the ramekins.*
3. *In a small bowl, stir together the caramel, salt, vanilla, liqueur if desired and butter.*
4. *Divide this mixture and pour over the bananas in each ramekin.*
5. *Cover each ramekin with a piece of aluminum foil.*
6. *Fill water tank with water.*
7. *Place the ramekins in steamer basket(s).*
8. *Cover steamer and set timer to 10 minutes.*
9. *When steaming is complete, carefully remove the ramekins and take off the foil.*
10. *Sprinkle each ramekin with the macadamia nuts and serve hot.*

TIP

It is normal for the bananas to take on a pinkish hue during steaming.

BABY FOOD

Makes 3-4 servings

EXTRAS

For the Beets Baby Food:

4 medium fresh beets

⅔ cups water (for the immersion chopper bowl)

For the Potato Baby Food:

4 medium potatoes, peeled and cubed

1 cup water (for the immersion chopper bowl)

For the Carrots Baby Food:

4 medium carrots, trimmed and peeled

⅔ cup water (for the immersion chopper bowl)

Method:

1. *Fill water tank with water.*
2. *Place the beets in the bottom steamer basket.*
3. *Place the potatoes in the middle steamer basket.*
4. *Place the carrots in the top steamer basket.*
5. *Put the basket with the beets on steamer.*
6. *Cover steamer and set timer to 30 minutes.*
7. *After 10 minutes, add the potato and carrot baskets to the steamer.*
8. *When steaming is complete, place each vegetable separately into an immersion chopper bowl and add the correct amount of water as stated above.*
9. *Pulse until smooth.*
10. *Serve immediately or freeze in individual containers for later use.*

BEET
MARMALADE

Makes 3 cups

Ingredients:

4 fresh beets

2 tablespoons fresh ginger, chopped

The zest and juice from a lemon

1½ cups granulated sugar

Method:

1. *If beets have tops, trim them off and save for another use or discard.*

2. *Place the beets in steamer basket(s).*

3. *Fill water tank with water.*

4. *Cover steamer and set timer to 30 minutes.*

5. *When steaming is complete, pierce beets with a small paring knife. If they are still hard, refill steamer with water and set timer for an additional 10 minutes or until beets are tender.*

6. *Remove and let cool.*

7. *Use gloves to peel off the skin from the beets.*

8. *Grate on large holes of a box grater or shred in a food processor.*

9. *Combine grated beets with remaining ingredients in a large saucepan over medium-high heat; bring to a full boil, stirring often.*

10. *Boil for 5 minutes or until slightly thickened.*

11. *Remove from heat and pour into storage containers or jars.*

12. *Let cool then refrigerate.*

13. *Marmalade will keep for 2 months in the refrigerator.*

TIP

This marmalade is wonderful served with poultry or spread on a turkey sandwich.

BOSTON BROWN BREAD

Makes 2 mini loaves

Ingredients:

¼ cup unbleached all purpose flour

½ cup 100% whole wheat flour

¼ cup rye flour

½ cup yellow cornmeal

1 teaspoon ground cinnamon

½ teaspoon kosher salt

½ teaspoon baking soda

1 cup buttermilk

⅓ cup molasses

½ cup dark raisins

Method:

1. *Apply nonstick spray to 2 canning jars that will fit inside the steamer baskets; set aside.*
2. *In a large mixing bowl, combine the flours, cornmeal, cinnamon, salt and baking soda; whisk using a hand whisk.*
3. *Whisk in remaining ingredients.*
4. *Spoon batter evenly into the prepared jars, filling them no more than 3/4 full.*
5. *Cover jars tightly with small squares of nonstick aluminum foil.*
6. *Fill water tank with water.*
7. *Place the jars in steamer basket(s).*
8. *Cover steamer and set timer to 25 minutes.*
9. *When steaming is complete, remove carefully and test for doneness by inserting a toothpick off-center. It should come out with just a few moist crumbs clinging to it (steam for an additional 5 minutes if needed).*
10. *Let cool for 1 hour before serving.*

EGG
NESTS

Makes 4 servings

Ingredients:

8 prosciutto slices

2 tablespoons unsalted butter, softened

2-4 slices Challah or other egg bread, toasted

4 large eggs

4 tablespoons half & half

Kosher salt and fresh pepper to taste

4 teaspoons fresh chives, minced

Method:

1. *Apply nonstick spray to four 4-ounce ramekins.*
2. *Line each ramekin with 2 slices of prosciutto, letting some hang over the edge.*
3. *Butter the toasted bread slices.*
4. *Use a 2-inch cookie cutter to cut out rounds from the bread.*
5. *Place a round of bread into each ramekin, pressing it down.*
6. *Crack an egg on top of each piece of bread.*
7. *Drizzle 1 tablespoon of half & half over each egg.*
8. *Season with salt and pepper.*
9. *Cover each ramekin with a small piece of aluminum foil.*
10. *Arrange the ramekins in steamer basket(s).*
11. *Fill water tank with water.*
12. *Cover steamer and set timer to 8 minutes.*
13. *Steam for 7-8 minutes for soft cooked eggs or until desired doneness.*
14. *When steaming is complete, carefully remove from steamer and discarding the foil.*
15. *Sprinkle each egg nest with chives and serve hot.*

EGGS STEAMED
IN TOMATOES

Makes 4 servings

Ingredients:

4 medium firm red tomatoes

Kosher salt and fresh pepper to taste

4 large eggs

¼ cup Parmesan cheese, grated

4 teaspoons extra-virgin olive oil

8 basil leaves, cut into thin ribbons

Method:

1. *Cut off the top ½-inch of each tomato.*
2. *Use a teaspoon or melon baller to remove the pulp from the centers (leave the tomato walls ½-thick).*
3. *Drain tomatoes upside down on a paper towel for 3 minutes.*
4. *Season the inside of each tomato generously with salt and pepper.*
5. *Crack an egg into each tomato and top each with some Parmesan cheese.*
6. *Fill water tank with water.*
7. *Place the tomatoes in steamer basket(s).*
8. *Cover steamer and set timer to 10 minutes.*
9. *Steam for 8-10 minutes for a runny yolk or add a minute if you prefer the yolk more done.*
10. *Remove carefully and serve with a drizzle of olive oil and basil.*

QUICK CHOW-CHOW RELISH

Makes 3 cups

For The Steamer:

½ head cauliflower, in florets

¼ head green cabbage, chopped

1 red bell pepper, diced

1 small yellow onion, diced

1 cucumber, diced

For The Brine:

2 tablespoons kosher salt

⅓ cup all purpose flour

2 tablespoons dry mustard

2 teaspoons turmeric

1½ cups granulated sugar

3 cups white vinegar

Method:

1. *Fill water tank with water.*
2. *Arrange all vegetables in steamer basket(s).*
3. *Cover steamer and set timer to 5 minutes.*
4. *When steaming is complete, remove immediately and set aside.*
5. *Combine all brine ingredients in a saucepan over medium-high heat.*
6. *Whisk constantly until mixture comes to a full boil and thickens.*
7. *Remove from heat.*
8. *Divide vegetables evenly between canning jars.*
9. *Pour brine over vegetables in the jars; cover and let cool.*
10. *Refrigerate before serving.*
11. *Chow-chow will keep, refrigerated for up to 2 months.*

SAVORY SPINACH & RICOTTA CUSTARD

Makes 4 servings

Ingredients:

Unsalted butter, for greasing

4 bay leaves

9 ounces frozen spinach, thawed and drained

3 fresh mint leaves, finely chopped

10 ounces ricotta cheese

2 large eggs

1 tablespoon fresh lime zest

Kosher salt and fresh pepper to taste

Method:

1. *Lightly butter the insides of 4 ramekins.*
2. *Place a bay leaf in the bottom of each ramekin.*
3. *In a bowl, combine remaining ingredients.*
4. *Spoon the mixture into the ramekins until 3/4 full.*
5. *Cover each ramekin with a piece of parchment paper then secure around the edge using a rubber band or a piece of string.*
6. *Place the ramekins in steamer basket(s).*
7. *Cover steamer and set timer to 18 minutes.*
8. *Steam for 16-18 minutes or until set.*
9. *When steaming is complete, remove and let cool for 5 minutes.*
10. *Flip ramekins upside-down on a plate then lift to remove the custard.*
11. *Garnish as desired and serve.*

TIP

You can use fresh spinach by steaming the spinach for 3-4 minutes or until wilted and remove as much water as possible.

STUFFED PEPPERS

Makes 4 servings

Ingredients:

2 cups rice, cooked

1 cup tomatoes, finely chopped

1 small onion, finely chopped

3 green onions, chopped

1 teaspoon lemon zest

2 tablespoons fresh lemon juice

2 tablespoons olive oil

2 teaspoons kosher salt

4 large green bell peppers, tops removed and cored

Method:

1. *In a bowl, combine all ingredients, except bell peppers.*
2. *Trim off the bottom of the bell peppers so they sit flat.*
3. *Spoon the rice mixture into the bell peppers and pack tightly.*
4. *Fill water tank with water.*
5. *Place the bell peppers in steamer basket(s).*
6. *Cover steamer and set timer to 20 minutes.*
7. *Steam for 18-20 minutes or until bell peppers are tender and filling is hot.*
8. *When steaming is complete, remove using tongs and serve.*

TOASTED CORNMEAL CORNBREAD

Makes 6 servings

Ingredients:

2¼ cups yellow cornmeal

⅓ cup unsalted butter, melted

1 tablespoon granulated sugar

1 teaspoon baking soda

1 teaspoon baking powder

1 teaspoon kosher salt

2 large eggs

Method:

1. Preheat oven to 350 °F.
2. Spread the cornmeal out onto a cookie sheet.
3. Bake cornmeal for 8-10 minutes or until brown and nutty smelling; remove and let cool.
4. Apply nonstick spray to 6 mini loaf pans or silicone molds; set aside.
5. In a mixing bowl, combine remaining ingredients; whisk until just smooth.
6. Pour batter into the molds, filling each until 2/3 full.
7. Cover tops with small squares of nonstick aluminum foil.
8. Fill water tank with water.
9. Place the molds in steamer basket(s).
10. Cover steamer and set timer to 15 minutes.
11. Steam for 15 minutes then test for doneness by inserting a toothpick off-center, it should come out with just a few moist crumbs clinging to it.
12. When steaming is complete, remove and serve.

SOURCE PAGE

Here are some of my favorite places to find ingredients that are not readily available at grocery stores as well as kitchen tools and supplies that help you become a better cook.

Chocosphere

P.O. Box 2237
Tualatin, OR 97062
877-992-4623

Excellent quality cocoa (Callebaut)
All Chocolates
Jimmies and sprinkles
www.chocosphere.com

D & G Occasions

625 Herndon Ave.
Orlando, FL 32803
407-894-4458

My favorite butter vanilla extract by Magic Line, cake and candy making supplies, citric acid, pure fruit oils, professional food colorings, ultra thin flexible spatulas, large selection of sprinkles and jimmies, unusual birthday candles, pure vanilla extract, pastry bags and tips, parchment, off-set spatulas, oven and candy thermometers, kitchen timers
www.dandgoccasions.com

Fortune Products, Inc.

205 Hickory Creek Road
Marble Falls, TX 78654
830-693-6111

Inexpensive, hand-held Accusharp knife sharpeners
www.accusharp.com

Rolling Pin Kitchen Emporium

P.O. Box 21798
Long Beach, CA 90801
949-221-9399

Cheesecloth, inexpensive "harp" shaped vegetable peelers, measuring cups and spoons, knives, vast array of kitchen tools including microplane graters, blow torches, baking pans and dishes
www.rollingpin.com

Penzeys Spices

P.O. Box 924
Brookfield, WI 53045
800-741-7787

Spices, extracts, seasonings and more
www.penzeys.com

Nui Enterprises

501 Chapala St. Suite A
Santa Barbara, CA 93101
805-965-5153

Vanilla from Tahiti
www.vanillafromtahiti.com

Whole Foods

550 Bowie St.
Austin, TX 78703
512-477-4455

Grains, citric acid, natural and organic
products, xanthan gum, gluten-free
baking items, real truffle oil,
miso paste
www.wholefoods.com

Gluten Free Mall

4927 Sonoma HWY Suite C1
Santa Rosa, CA 95409
707-509-4528

All ingredients needed for gluten-free baking
www.glutenfreemall.com

The Bakers Catalogue at King Arthur Flour

135 Route 5 South
P.O. Box 1010
Norwich, VT 05055

Pure fruit oils, citric acid, silicone spatulas,
digital timers, oven thermometers, real truffle
oil, off-set spatulas, measuring cups and
spoons, knives, ice cream scoops, cheesecloth,
microplane graters, cookie sheets, baking pans
www.kingarthurflour.com